Fabulous
FOOD ART

First published in Australia by Serenity Press Pty Ltd, 2024

Text copyright © Sarah Ferguson 2024
Art copyright © Laleh Mohmedi 2024

A CIP catalogue record for this book is available from the National Library of Australia
ISBN: 978-0-9954104-8-0

Serenity Press books may be ordered through online booksellers or by contacting:
www.serenitypress.org
publisher@serenitypress.org

Contents

BREAKFAST

Mice Stack
SPELT PANCAKES

TIME
30 min

SERVES
4 People

DIFFICULTY
Easy

INGREDIENTS

PANCAKES

**2 CUPS OF SPELT FLOUR 225G • 1 TSP BAKING POWDER • 1 CUP MILK 225ML
2 EGGS • 3 TBSP HONEY • BUTTER**

MICE

4 STRAWBERRIES • 4 BLUEBERRIES • BLACK PANCAKE

RECIPE

Pancake

1. Place all the pancake ingredients in a bowl and mix to create the pancake batter.
2. Heat up a pan and place butter till it melts.
3. Place small amounts of pancake batter, ½ a ladleful, onto the pan. Slightly lift the pancake, once it is golden brown flip and cook the other side.
4. Stack the pancakes on top of each other. Pour a small amount of honey on top if desired.

CREATION METHOD

1. Cut the bottom of a strawberry so that it can sit flat without wobbling.
2. Using a knife, cut two ear shapes out of the slice of strawberry.
3. Using a large marker lid, cut two circles out of a pancake – these will be used for the eyes.
4. Using a knife cut two slices out of a blueberry – these will be used for the iris.
5. Using a pen lid cut two circles out of a black pancake – these will be used for the pupils.
6. Using the mini circle cutter cut two circles out of the pancake – these will be used to create an element of shine to the eye.
7. Place the blue iris onto of the pancake eye, place the pupil onto the iris, place the small pancake shine on the left side of each eye. These elements should all naturally stick together – in the case that they don't use a little bit of honey as glue.
8. Using a knife cut two slits on the top of the strawberry and insert one ear in each slit.
9. Using honey stick the two eyes on to the strawberry.
10. Place a toothpick in the blueberry and insert it into the strawberry below the eyes for the nose
11. Place the mice around onto of the stack. Place small amounts of pancake batter ½ a ladleful onto the pan. Slightly lift the pancake, once it is golden brown flip and cook the other side
12. Stack the pancakes on top of each other. Pour a small amount of honey on top if desired.

Sarah Says

Ooh how nice for the mice yum yum snacks for a delicious mice stack!

Genie Gems
DRAGON TOAST

TIME
15 min

SERVES
1+ People

DIFFICULTY
Easy

INGREDIENTS

I QUAIL EGG • I SLICE OF WHOLEMEAL BREAD • I AVOCADO • I SMALL CUCUMBER • BLACK PANCAKE

CREATION METHOD

1. Boil a quail egg in a pot of water, once the egg is cooked remove it from the pot and place in cold water.
2. Toast bread.
3. Slice avocado in half.
4. Using a knife cut out two ears and a neck out of the other half of the avocado.
5. Using a knife cut triangles out of the cucumber to create the spikes.
6. Using scissors cut around the edge of the black pancake – this will be used as the mouth.
7. Using scissors cut two small lines for the eyebrows out of the black pancake.
8. Using the small circle cutter cut two circles out of the remaining black pancake – these will be used for the pupils.
9. Peel the quail egg and cut in half – these will be used as the eyes.
10. Place the avocado half onto the toast.
11. Place the avocado ears onto of the head.
12. Place the neck on the right side of the head.
13. Place the quail eggs on to the face.
14. Place the black pancake pupils on each of the quail eyes.
15. Place the eyebrows on top of each eye.
16. Place the black pancake mouth from the bottom of the avocado to the bottom of the eye.
17. Place the cucumber spikes above the neck.

Genie Gems
PRINCESS TOAST

TIME
15 min

SERVES
1+ People

DIFFICULTY
Easy

INGREDIENTS

HOMEMADE HUMMUS • 1/2 RED CAPSICUM • 1/4 YELLOW CAPSICUM • 1 CUCUMBER

1 QUAIL EGG • BLACK PANCAKE • 1 SLICE OF WHOLEMEAL BREAD

CREATION METHOD

1. Boil a quail egg in a pot of water until hard boiled, once the egg is cooked remove it from the pot and place in cold water.

2. Toast bread.

3. Using a knife cut the shape of the hair (use image as reference) out of a red capsicum.

4. Using a knife cut the shape of a crown out of a yellow capsicum.

5. Using a knife cut a tiny diamond shape out of the cucumber.

6. Bend a straw so that it is a slight oval shape and cut two ovals out of the black pancake – these will be used for the eyes.

7. Using scissors cut a small Line for the nose.

8. Peel the quail egg, using a knife cut a crescent shape – this will be used for the mouth.

9. Place a dollop of hummus onto the centre of toast. Using a spoon spread in circular motion to create a circle shape.

10. Place the capsicum hair onto the the hummus.

11. Place the eyes below the hair.

12. Place the nose in between the eyes.

13. Place the mouth below the nose.

14. Place the yellow capsicum crown above the head, place the cucumber diamond in the middle of the crown.

Genie Gems
DEVON SCONES

TIME
20 min

SERVES
6

DIFFICULTY
Easy

INGREDIENTS

350G SELF-RAISING FLOUR • TSP BAKING POWDER • 85G BUTTER • 3 TBSP CASTER SUGAR
175ML BUTTERMILK • 1 TSP VANILLA EXTRACT • BEATEN EGG • 3 TBSP OF DOUBLE CREAM •
1 STRAWBERRY • 1 SLICE OF PINEAPPLE • 10 BLUEBERRIES • BLACK PANCAKE

RECIPE

1. Preheat oven to 220c.
2. Place self-raising flour, salt and baking powder into a large bowl and mix.
3. Add the butter, then rub in with your fingers until the mix looks like breadcrumbs.
4. Add the caster sugar.
5. Warm the buttermilk in a pan for a couple of minutes until warm, but not hot.
6. Add vanilla extract to the buttermilk then mix into the flour mixture.
7. Put some flour onto a work surface and pat the dough out to approx 4 cm depth.
8. Using a circle cutter, cut 6 scones out of the dough.
9. Brush the tops with a beaten egg and a sprinkling of sugar then put on a baking tray.
10. Bake for 10 mins until risen and golden on the top.

CREATION METHOD

1. In a small bowl squash some blueberries into a small amount of cream and mix to create a greyish colour.
2. Spread the plain cream all over the scone.
3. Place some of the greyish cream at the tip to create the snout – you can layer the cream to make an oval shape.
4. Slightly squeeze a straw to create an oval shape, cut two ovals out of the black pancake.
5. Using scissors cut two lines around the edge of the black pancake – these will be used to create the eye shape.
6. Using a knife cut a horn shape out of a slice of pineapple.
7. Using a knife cut a few slices of strawberry – this will be used for the mane.
8. Cut the blueberries in quarters – these will also be used for the mane.
9. Place the eyes towards the top of the scone, place the two lines above each eye and slightly curve.
10. Place the pineapple horn into the scone so that it is sticking out.
11. Place the blueberries around the pineapple.
12. Place the strawberry mane on the side.

Macaw
CREAM CHEESE & FRUIT

TIME
10 min

SERVES
1⁺ People

DIFFICULTY
Intermediate

INGREDIENTS

STRAWBERRIES • CREAM CHEESE • FLATBREAD • BLUEBERRIES • CUCUMBER • PINEAPPLE • BLACK PANCAKE

CREATION METHOD

1. Using scissors cut a round arch shape out of the flatbread.
2. Using a straw cut a circle out of remaining flatbread – this will be used for the shine element of the eye.
3. Using a knife cut the tip off a small cucumber, then cut the bottom to create a small round arch shape – this will be used for the iris.
4. Using an extra-large pen lid cut a circle out of a black pancake – this will be used for the pupil.
5. With the remainder of the black pancake cut a beak shape – refer to image.
6. Using scissors cut along the edge of the black pancake – cut a few smaller pieces – these will be used to outline the eye and eyelashes.
7. Using a knife cut a few strawberries in quarters – these will be used for the crescent.
8. Using a knife cut a few slices out of a cucumber and pineapple.
9. Using a spoon place the cream cheese in the centre of the plate, spread in a circular motion.
10. Place the quarter slices around the cream cheese face and then a curved line down towards the bottom of the plate – this will create the body shape.
11. Place the pineapple slice on top of the strawberry slices.
12. Place the cucumber on top of the pineapple slice.
13. Place full strawberries along the other side of the body – making sure to leave a space between the cucumber slice and strawberries.
14. Place blueberries in between the cucumber and strawberries.
15. Place the round arched flatbread in the centre of the cream cheese.
16. Place the cucumber round arch on the bottom of the flatbread so that the bottom aligns with he flatbread.
17. Place the black pancake round arch onto the cucumber, again aligning the bottoms.
18. Place the tiny flatbread circle in the middle of the black pancake pupil.
19. Using tweezers carefully place the black pancake line along the edge of the flatbread round arch making sure the end curls to create an eyelash, place another eyelash below the curved line.
20. Place a strawberry on the right-hand side of the cream cheese, place the bottom of the beak on top of the strawberry, place the top of the black pancake beak above the bottom piece.

Genie Gems
OMELETTES

TIME
25 min

SERVES
8-10 Omlettes

DIFFICULTY
Easy

INGREDIENTS

4 EGGS • 1 CUP GRATED CHEESE • 1 ONION • 1/2 CUP SPINACH • 1/3 CUP MILK • 1/2 CUP SLICED MUSHROOMS • SEA SALT (OPTIONAL) • OLIVE OIL/BUTTER • YELLOW CAPSICUM • FLATBREAD BLACK PANCAKE • SAUTÉED MUSHROOMS

RECIPE

1. Preheat oven to 180c.
2. Dice onions and mushrooms.
3. Place a bit of olive oil or butter onto a pan, add onion and mushroom. Cook until they are sautéed.
4. In a bowl add eggs, cheese, spinach, milk and mix.
5. Once onion and mushroom have cooled down place in batter, keeping some mushrooms aside for later.
6. Add a pinch of salt (optional).
7. Use olive oil or butter to grease a cupcake tray.
8. Fill each cupcake with omelette batter.
9. Place in oven for 8-10 minutes or until golden brown.
10. Using a knife cut a crown shape and ribbon out of the yellow capsicum.

11. Using an oval shaped cutter cut two ovals out of the flatbread – these will be used for the eyes.
12. Using the tiny circle cutter cut two circles out of the black pancake – these will be used for the pupils.
13. Using scissors cut along the edge of the pancake – this will be used for the mouth.
14. Layer the sautéed mushrooms on the top half of the omelette.
15. Place the two oval shape flatbreads onto the omelette.
16. Place the black pancake pupils on each of the eyes.
17. Place the black pancake mouth below the eyes.
18. Place the crown above the eyes.
19. Place the yellow capsicum ribbon on the bottom left side of the crown.

Beachy
SCRAMBLED EGGS

TIME	**SERVES**	**DIFFICULTY**
20 min	1+ People	Intermediate

INGREDIENTS

2 EGGS • DASH OF MILK • 1/4 CUP GRATED CHEESE • 1 SLICE OF BREAD • CUCUMBER • YELLOW CAPSICUM CARROT • RED CAPSICUM • BLACK PANCAKE • YOGHURT • BLUE SPIRULINA • BUTTER

CREATION RECIPE

1. In a small bowl mix the eggs and milk.
2. Place a small amount of butter into a pan and allow to melt.
3. Add the eggs and gently stir until fluffy.
4. Evenly mix in the cheese.
5. Using a large pen lid cut 5 circles out of the bread.
6. Using a knife cut 4 leaf shapes out of the cucumber.
7. Using a small circle cutter cut a circle out of the yellow capsicum – this will be used to create the sun.
8. Using a knife cut a castle out of the yellow capsicum, cut a few strips with the remainder of the capsicum – these will be used for the sun's rays.
9. Using a knife cut a bucket and spade shape out of the red capsicum – refer to image.
10. Using a knife cut a few smaller strips of the red capsicum – this will also be used for the sun's rays.
11. Using a tiny circle cutter cut two circles out of the remainder of the red capsicum – this will be used for the sun's cheeks.
12. Using a straw cut two circles out of the black pancake – these will be used for the sun's eyes.
13. Using scissors cut along the edge of the black pancake to create the sun's mouth.
14. In a small bowl add some yoghurt and blue spirulina and mix until blue.
15. Using a spoon spread the yoghurt onto the plate to create waves – refer to image.
16. Place the scrambled eggs below the yoghurt to create the sand.
17. Place the bread circles in a curved line to create the tree, add the cucumber leaves.
18. Place the yellow capsicum sun above the yoghurt, add the red and yellow capsicum to create the sun's rays.
19. Place the black pancake eyes on to the yellow capsicum.
20. Place the white flatbread circles to the left side of each eye to create an element of shine.
21. Place the red capsicum cheeks below each eye.
22. Place the black pancake mouth below the eyes.
23. Place the sandcastle yellow capsicum and red capsicum bucket and spade onto the eggs.

Monkey
OAT CAKE MUFFIN

TIME
45 min

SERVES
1+ People

DIFFICULTY
Easy

INGREDIENTS

I CUP OATS • I EGG • I/2 CUP MILK • ITSP BAKING POWDER • I BANANA • 2 TBSP CHIA SEEDS
I/4 CUP RAW HONEY • STRAWBERRY • PEANUT BUTTER • COCOA POWDER • BANANA
BLACK PANCAKE • SULTANA • FLATBREAD

RECIPE

1. Preheat oven to 180c.
2. Add oats into a processor and blitz until oat flour is formed.
3. Add egg, milk, baking powder, banana, chia seeds, honey into the processor and blitz until a batter is formed.
4. Using some baking paper grease a ramekin with some butter or coconut oil.
5. Pour batter into the ramekin and place in oven for 25-30 minutes – make sure it is completely cooked through before removing from oven.
6. Whilst the muffins are cooking using a pen lid cut two circles out of a black pancake – these will be used for the eyes.

CREATION METHOD

1. Using scissors cut along the edge of the black pancake to create a mouth. Cut two smaller lines for the eyebrows.
2. Using a tiny circle cutter cut two circles out of the flat pancake these will be used to create an element of shine in the eye.

3. Using a knife slice the tip of a strawberry to create two oval shapes – these will be used for the cheeks.
4. In a small bowl add some peanut butter and cocoa powder and mix to create a smooth consistency.
5. In a seperate bowl place a banana and smoosh it up with a fork.
6. Once the cake has cooled down, using a spoon spread the banana on top.
7. Using a separate spoon place the chocolate spread around the top of the head – refer to image.
8. Place the black pancake eyes on to the face.
9. Place the tiny circle flatbread on the left side of each pupil.
10. Place the strawberry cheeks below each eye.
11. Place the sultana nose in between the cheeks.
12. Place the black pancake eyebrows above each eye.
13. Optional – to make the ears cut two ear shapes out of the another muffin and cover with cocoa spread.

Aerolina
SAVOURY MUFFINS

TIME
50 min

SERVES
12 People

DIFFICULTY
Intermediate

INGREDIENTS

2 CUPS SPELT FLOUR • 1 TSP BAKING POWDER • 1 CUP MILK • 2 EGGS • 1 ONION • 1/2 CUP GRATED ZUCCHINI
1/2 GRATED PUMPKIN • 1 CUP SPINACH • 1 CUP GRATED CHEESE • 1/2 CUP GRATED CARROT • 1/4 CUP HONEY
BLUEBERRIES • BLACK PANCAKE • CREAM CHEESE • YELLOW CAPSICUM • FLATBREAD

RECIPE

1. Preheat oven to 180c.
2. Add some olive oil onto a frying pan, add diced onions and cook until brown.
3. In a large bowl add flour, milk, baking powder, honey, eggs and mix until a smooth consistency.
4. Gently fold in the zucchini, pumpkin, carrot, spinach and grated cheese.
5. Grease a muffin pan and pour in the muffin batter.
6. Place in oven for 30-35 minutes.

CREATION METHOD

1. Using a small oval cutter cut two ovals out of the flatbread – this will be used for the eyes.
2. Using a tiny circle cutter cut two circles out of the black pancake – these will be used for the pupils.
3. Using scissors cut around the edge of the pancake to create six lines.
4. Using scissors cut a beak shape out of the remaining black pancake.
5. Using a knife cut the curved strip out of the yellow capsicum.
6. Once the muffin has cooled place desired amount of cream cheese to cover the muffin.
7. Place the flatbread eyes in the centre of the muffin.
8. Place the tiny circle black pancake pupil onto the eye.
9. Place the black pancake beak below the eyes.
10. Place two black pancake lines underneath each eye.
11. Place one black pancake line above each eye to create the eyebrows.
12. Place a few blueberries around the top of the head to create feathers.
13. Place the yellow capsicum strip below the beak.

Little Boy Blue
PORRIDGE

TIME
15 min

SERVES
1 People

DIFFICULTY
Easy

INGREDIENTS

1/2 CUP OATS • 1 CUP MILK • 1/2 CUP WATER • 2 TBSP RAW HONEY • 1 TSP CHIA SEEDS • PINEAPPLE • BLUEBERRIES • BLACK PANCAKE • ALMONDS • YOGHURT • RASPBERRY • SHAVED COCONUT

RECIPE

1. Add oats, water, milk and chia into a pot and allow to cook, make sure to stir continuously.
2. Add in honey and mix through.

CREATION METHOD

1. Whilst porridge is cooking using a knife cut a round arch shape to create the cap.
2. Using a knife cut an oval shape out of remaining pineapple – this will be used for the bee.
3. Slightly squeeze a pen lid and cut two oval shapes out of the black pancake – this will be used for the eyes.
4. Using a larger pen lid, cut another oval shape out of the black pancake to create the mouth.
5. Using a tiny circle cutter cut one circle – this will create the eye for the bee.
6. Using scissors cut around the edge of the black pancake – this will be used for the mouth.
7. Using scissors cut two smaller lines to create the eyebrows.
8. In small bowl add a spoon of yoghurt, squash one raspberry into the yoghurt and mix to create a pink colour – this will be used for the cheeks.

9. Pour porridge into a bowl, starting from the top of the bowl place shredded coconut in a line.
10. To create the hat place blueberries below the coconut, place another line of coconut below the blueberries and another line of blueberries below the coconut, this time only going halfway.
11. Insert the pineapple next to the strip of blueberries.
12. Place a line of almonds below the blueberries/pineapple to create the hair .
13. Place the black pancake eyes below the almonds.
14. Place the black pancake line in between the eyes making sure it is slightly curved to create the nose.
15. Place one small black pancake line above each eye.
16. Place the large oval black pancake below the nose.
17. Place the pineapple oval on the top of the hat, slice a blueberry in half and place it onto the pineapple.
18. Add the tiny black pancake circle on the right side of the oval to create the eye.
19. Add two almond slithers onto of the bumble bee to create the bee's wings.
20. Using a teaspoon place a small amount of yoghurt under each eye to create the cheeks.

LUNCH

Panda
SUSHI BALLS

TIME
30 min

SERVES
People

DIFFICULTY
Intermediate

INGREDIENTS

I CUP GLUTINOUS RICE • I CAN TUNA • I CUCUMBER • I CARROT • I AVOCADO • NORI • CUCUMBER • PICKLED GINGER • FLATBREAD • BLACK PANCAKE

CREATION METHOD

1. Wash rice, then pour into pot and fill with water. Make sure water is 1/4 of a finger above the rice, place on low heat and allow to cook.

2. Using a large pen cut two circles out of the flatbread.

3. Slice the end of the cucumber to create two circles – this will be used for the iris.

4. Using a straw cut two circles out of the black pancake, this will be used for the pupils.

5. Using scissors cut a triangle shape out of the remaining pancake.

6. Using scissors cut two lines out of the pancake.

7. Using scissors cut two round arch shapes out of a sheet of nori – this will be used for the eye patches.

8. Using scissors cut two ovals out of a pickled ginger - this will be used for the cheeks.

9. Once the rice is cooked, allow it to cool down. Then place a few tablespoons onto a piece of cling wrap. Using a spoon spread the rice into a circular shape.

10. Place tuna, cucumber, avocado or any filling that you wish in the middle of the rice.

11. Pick up each edge of the cling wrap and bring them together. Twist the edges together to create a rice ball. Mould the rice into an oval. This will be used for the panda's head.

12. Cut two small squares of cling wrap, place a teaspoon of rice in the middle and again bring the edges together and twist so that they look like two little balls – these will be used to create the ears.

13. Using scissors cut two squares of nori, make sure they are larger than the ears. Remove the cling wrap from the balls and gently wrap them with the nori.

14. Remove the cling wrap from the head and place onto a plate.

15. Place the round arched piece of nori onto the rice ball.

16. Place the flatbread circle onto the nori patches.

17. Place the cucumber slice irises onto the flatbread.

18. Place the black pancake pupils onto the cucumber.

19. Place the tiny circle flatbread onto the left side of each pupil to create an element of shine.

20. Place the black pancake triangle nose in between the eyes.

21. Place one black pancake line vertically below the nose and another horizontally at the bottom of the other line to create the mouth, making sure to slightly curve it to create a smile.

22. Place one piece of pickled ginger below each eye for the cheeks.

23. Place the ears above the head.

Feta & Spinach
SNAIL SCROLLS

TIME	**SERVES**	**DIFFICULTY**
45 min	8 People	Intermediate

INGREDIENTS

2 CUPS SELF-RAISING FLOUR • I CUP PLAIN YOGHURT • I CUP SPINACH • I CUP GRATED CHEESE

FLATBREAD • CUCUMBER • BLACK PANCAKE

RECIPE

I. Preheat over to 180c.

2. Place flour and yoghurt into bowl and gently mix until you create a dough-like texture.

3. Dust some flour onto a bench and knead the dough for a few minutes. If you find that the dough is sticky add a little more flour.

4. Roll the dough into a bowl and then roll flat using a rolling pin.

5. Spread cheese and spinach.

6. Gently roll the dough from one edge towards the other, but do not roll all the way as you will need this to create the face.

7. Cut the dough into 8 pieces.

8. Slightly shape the end that was not rolled to create the head.

9. Place onto tray and in the oven for 20 minutes.

CREATION METHOD

I. Using scissors cut two strips out of the flatbread to create antennas, place in oven until they are golden brown.

2. Using a large pen lid slightly squeeze into an oval shape and cut two ovals out of the flatbread – this will be used to create the eyes.

3. Using a tiny circle cutter cut two circles out of the remaining flatbread – this will be used to create an element of shine in the eyes.

4. Using a knife cut the tip off a small cucumber – these will be used to create the iris. If you can not find a small cucumber use a small pen lid to cut to circles out of a slice of cucumber.

5. Using a straw but two circles out of a pancake – this will be used to create the pupils.

6. Once the scrolls are cooked and cooled down a little insert the antennas into the head.

7. Place the flatbread eyes onto the head.

8. Place cucumber iris onto each eye.

9. Place the black pancake pupil onto the iris.

I0. Place the tiny flatbread circles onto the left side of each eye to create an element of shine.

Giraffe
CORN FRITTERS

TIME
45 min

SERVES
6 People

DIFFICULTY
Intermediate

INGREDIENTS

2 CUPS CORN KERNELS • 2 EGGS • 1/2 CUP DICED SPINACH • 1/2 CUP GRATED CHEESE • 1/4 CUP CORN FLOUR
OLIVE OIL • MUSHROOMS • ASPARAGUS • CUCUMBER • FLATBREAD • BLACK PANCAKE

RECIPE

1. Place corn kernels, eggs, spinach, cheese and corn flour in a large bowl and mix until all the ingredients are combined.

2. Heat some oil in a frying pan and add some of the mixture, gently spread to create an oval shape. Using a teaspoon place small amounts of the mixture to create the ear shapes. If you find this too difficult to create the ear shapes you can cut them out of a fritter once they are cooked.

3. Once one side is golden brown, flip the fritter to cook the other.

4. Once cooked place on paper towel to remove the excess oil.

CREATION METHOD

1. Slice some mushrooms and sauté in a pan with some olive oil until golden brown.

2. Sauté two stalks of asparagus – these will be used for the antennas.

3. Using scissors cut two large oval shapes out of flatbread – these will be used to create the eyes.

4. Using a straw cut two circles out of a remaining flatbread – these will be used to create an element of shine in the eye.

5. Using a knife cut two smaller oval out of a slice of cucumber – these will be used to for the iris.

6. Using scissors cut two even small oval shapes out of a black pancake – these will be used for the pupils.

7. Using scissors cut around the edge of the pancake to create two thick strips – this will be used to create the outline of the eye.

8. Using scissors cut two smaller strips – these will be used for the nostrils.

9. To create the snout gently layer the sautéed mushrooms from the bottom of the fritter to 1/4 of the way up.

10. Place the flatbread eyes on each side of the fritter.

11. Place the cucumber irises on to the flatbread making sure it is placed towards the inner side.

12. Place the black pancake pupils into the cucumber.

13. Place the small flatbread circles on the left side of each black pancake pupil.

14. Using tweezers gently place the black pancake strips along the edge of the eyes, slightly curving them at the end to create an eyelash.

15. Place the two strips onto the mushrooms to create the nostrils.

16. Add the ears on top of the head.

17. Place the asparagus antenna in the middle of the ears.

Sarah Says

Giraffe, yum you make me laugh. You see so clearly, high up above the tree.

Monster
POTATO & PEA FRITTERS

TIME	SERVES	DIFFICULTY
45 min	8-10 Fritters	Intermediate

INGREDIENTS

4 POTATOES • I CUP PEAS • I/2 CUP DICED SPINACH • I EGG • I TSP SALT • I/2 CUP GRATED ZUCCHINI
CRÈME FRAÎCHE • CUCUMBER • SMOKED SALMON • FLATBREAD • BLACK PANCAKE

RECIPE

1. Peel potatoes and cut them into cubes, place in pot of water and cook until potatoes are soft.
2. Once potatoes are cooked strain and place in a large bowl and mash them until a smooth consistency.
3. Add peas, spinach, egg, grated zucchini and salt into bowl and mix until combined.
4. Using your hand scoop a small handful of the mixture and roll into a ball, then gently flatten the bowl.
5. Place olive oil in a pan, once the oil has heated gently place the fritter onto the pan and allow to cook. Once golden brown flip to the other side. Once cooked on both sides place on paper towel.

CREATION METHOD

1. Using a small circle cutter cut two circles out of a flatbread – this will be used for the eyes.
2. Using a tiny circle cutter cut two circles out of the flatbread – this will be used to create an element of shine.
3. Using scissors cut two small triangles out of the remaining flatbread – these will be used for the teeth. `

4. Using a knife slice the ends of a small cucumber to create two circles – this will be used for the iris.
5. Using a knife cut two horn shapes out of the remaining cucumber – refer to image.
6. Using a pen lid cut two circles out of a black pancake these will be used for the pupils.
7. Using scissors cut along the edge of the black pancake to create a strip.
8. Using scissors cut a small triangle out of some smoked salmon.
9. Using a teaspoon place a small amount of crème fraîche onto the flatbread circle – making sure to cover it.
10. Place the eyes onto the fritter.
11. Place the cucumber iris onto the eyes.
12. Place the black pancake pupils onto the cucumber.
13. Place the little flatbread circles onto the left side of each pupil.
14. Place the smoked salmon triangle below the eyes – make sure that the triangle is upside down.
15. Place the black pancake strip below the nose.
16. Place one triangle flatbread on each end of the mouth.
17. Place cucumber horns above the fritter.

Rainbow
PIZZAS

TIME
90 min

SERVES
3 Pizzas

DIFFICULTY
Intermediate

INGREDIENTS

375 ML WARM WATER • 2 TSP INSTANT YEAST • 4 CUPS SPELT FLOUR • 1/4 CUP OLIVE OLIVE OIL PASSATA SAUCE • 1/2 CUP RED CAPSICUM • 1/2 CUP YELLOW CAPSICUM • 1/2 CUP SPINACH 1/4 PURPLE CABBAGE • BOCCONCINI CHEESE • 1 SMALL ONION

RECIPE

Dough

1. Combine water and yeast in a bowl and whisk until foamy.
2. Place flour in a large bowl, create a well in the middle and add the yeast mixture and oil.
3. Gently fold the mixture until all ingredients are combined. Once combined use your hands to create a dough. You may want to dust your hand with some flour first to avoid the dough sticking.
4. Dust your bench with some flour and knead the dough for 10 minutes.
5. Place the dough back into a bowl and cover with a tea towel. Set aside in a warm place and allow it to rise for 30 minutes.
6. Re-dust the bench with flour and form the dough into a long tube. Divide into 3 sections.
7. Using a rolling pin roll each section into a disc.
8. Preheat oven to 180c.

CREATION METHOD

1. Dice the onion. In a pan add some olive oil and fry the onion until soft. Add the passata sauce, 1/4 cup water and a pinch of salt – cook until sauce has reduced.
2. Dice the red capsicum, yellow capsicum and purple cabbage.
3. Using a spoon spread the sauce evenly onto the dough.
4. Place the red capsicum onto the pizza in an arch shape
5. Place the yellow capsicum below the red capsicum arch.
6. Allow a gap in between the yellow capsicum and the purple cabbage as the spinach will be placed there once pizza has been cooked.
7. Place bocconcini at the end of the vegetables to create the clouds.
8. Place in oven and allow to cook for 25 minutes.
9. Once pizza has been removed from the oven place the fresh spinach in between the yellow capsicum and purple cabbage.

Rosie Ballerina
SANDWICH

TIME
10 min

SERVES
1 People

DIFFICULTY
Easy

INGREDIENTS

1 SLICE OF BREAD • 2 TBSP CREAM CHEESE • DROP BEETROOT JUICE • 1 CHERRY TOMATO
1 SMALL CUCUMBER • 1 CARROT • BLACK PANCAKE

CREATION METHOD

1. Using a peeler, peel a carrot and place it in a bowl of water with ice – this will curl the carrot slices.

2. Using a large cookie cutter cut a circle out of the bread – this will be used for the face.

3. In small bowl mix the cream cheese and a drop of beetroot juice to create a light pink colour.

4. Using a large pen lid, slightly squeeze and cut out two oval shapes out of the black pancakes – these will be used for the eyes.

5. Using scissors cut along the edge of the pancake, cut one long strip for the mouth and three small strips for the nose, eyebrow and the other section of the mouth.

6. Using a knife cut the cherry tomato in half – these will be used for the cheeks.

7. Using a knife cut a slice of cucumber – this will be used for the headband.

8. Spread the cream cheese over the bread.

9. Place the black pancake eyes onto the bread towards the top of the head.

10. Place the small black pancake strip in between and below the eyes, making sure it is slightly curved.

11. Place the larger black pancake strip on a slight curved angle – refer to image. Place a small strip above to create the mouth.

12. Place the last small strip of black pancake above the left eye.

13. Place the cherry tomato cheeks below each eye.

14. Remove the carrot slices from the water and dry off in a paper towel. Place the carrot around the face to create the hair.

15. Place the cucumber slice headband on a slight angle on the top of the carrot hair.

Little Red
BEAR PIE

TIME
50 min

SERVES
4 People

DIFFICULTY
Intermediate

INGREDIENTS

4 SHEETS PUFF PASTRY • 500G MINCED BEEF • 1 ONION • 1 CUP PEAS • 1 CUP SPINACH • 1 CUP BEEF STOCK 1 TBSP CORN FLOUR • SALT • BLACK PANCAKE • OLIVE OIL

RECIPE

1. Preheat oven to 180c.
2. Dice onions and place in pot with some olive oil.
3. Once onion has browned add minced meat and brown.
4. Add the beef stock and salt and allow to simmer. Sprinkle some corn flour on top to thicken the sauce.
5. Stir in peas and spinach.
6. Using a pie shape cutter place the puff pastry on the bottom of the pie maker or ramekin.
7. Fill the ramekin with the the pie mixture.
8. Using a pie circle cutter cut a circle out of the pie and place on top of the ramekin.
9. Using scissors cut out two ear shapes out of the remaining puff pastry.
10. Place the pie and ears into the oven for 15 minutes or until pastry is golden brown.

CREATION METHOD

1. Using a pen lid slightly squeeze and cut two oval shapes out of the black pancake.
2. Using scissors cut along the edge of the black pancake to create a strip – this will be used for the mouth. Cut two smaller stripes – these will be used for the corner of the mouth and above the nose.
3. Using a knife cut a pitted olive in half and then cut it into a triangular shape.
4. Once the pie is cooked remove from the oven and place the black pancake eyes on to the pie.
5. Place the olive nose in below the eyes.
6. Place the larger black pancake strip mouth below the nose on an angle, place the smaller strip black pancake on top.
7. Place the remaining black pancake strip above the nose making sure it curves around the nose.
8. Using a knife make two incision in the pie above the eyes, insert the ears to that they are standing.

Little Red
BURGER BUN

TIME
30 min

SERVES
8 Buns

DIFFICULTY
Intermediate

INGREDIENTS

**2 TBSP ACTIVE DRY YEAST • I CUP WARM WATER • I/3 CUP OLIVE OIL • I EGG • I TSP SALT
4 CUPS WHOLEMEAL FLOUR • RED CAPSICUM • BLACK PANCAKE**

RECIPE

1. Combine water and yeast in a bowl and whisk until foamy.
2. Place flour in a large bowl, create a well in the middle and add the yeast mixture, oil and egg.
3. Gently fold the mixture until all ingredients are combined. Once combined use your hands to create a dough consistency. You may want to dust your hand with some flour first to avoid the dough sticking.
4. Dust your bench with some flour, place the dough onto the bench and knead for 2-3 minutes – do not let rise.
5. Divide the dough into 8 pieces, making sure to leave a small amount of dough aside for the nose.
6. Shape each part into a ball and place 6 cm apart on a greased baking tray.
7. Using the spare dough roll tiny little balls and place in the middle of the bun.
8. Bake for 12 minutes or until golden brown.
9. Remove the buns from the oven and allow to cool before cutting them in half. Fill the buns with meat patty of choice, lettuce, tomato, cheese and mayonnaise

CREATION METHOD

1. Using a knife cut a red capsicum in half. Cut out a hair shape.
2. Using a large pen lid, gently squeeze and cut two oval shapes out of a black pancake.
3. Using scissors cut around the edge of the pancake to create one large strip for the mouth and two smaller strips for the eyes.
4. Using a toothpick stick the hair on top of the bun.
5. Place the two black pancake eyes on either side of the nose.
6. Place the two smaller strips of black pancake above each eye.
7. Place the larger black pancake strip below the nose making sure it is curved to create a smile.

Sausage Dog
SAUSAGE ROLLS

TIME
90 min

SERVES
5 People

DIFFICULTY
Intermediate

INGREDIENTS

400G MINCED LAMB • 400G MINCED BEEF • 1 CARROT • 1 ONION • 1/2 CUP FINELY CHOPPED PARSLEY
1 TBSP TOMATO PASTE • 1 TBSP BBQ SAUCE • 1 TBSP WORCESTERSHIRE SAUCE • 5 SHEETS PUFF PASTRY
1 TSP SALT • 1 EGG • CUCUMBER • RED CAPSICUM • OLIVE • FLATBREAD • BLACK PANCAKE

RECIPE

1. Preheat oven to 160c.
2. Using a food processor grate the onion, carrot and parsley.
3. In a large bowl add the meat, onion, carrot, parsley, tomato paste, bbq sauce, Worcestershire sauce and salt – mix until all combined.
4. Cut each pastry sheet into four pieces.
5. Using your hands form the meat into a sausage shape in the middle of the puff pastry sheet.
6. Gently roll the puff pastry to create a cylinder, making sure to fold the front in to create the head of the dog.
7. Twist the end of the sausage roll to create a tail.
8. Using scissors cut two ears shapes out of the puff pastry.
9. Place sausage rolls and ears into the oven for 45 minutes or until golden brown.

CREATION METHOD

1. Using a large pen lid slightly bend it and cut two oval shapes out of the flatbread – these will be used to for the eyes.
2. Using a tiny circle cutter cut two circles in the remaining flatbread – these will be used to create an element of shine in the eye.
3. Using a large pen lid cut two circles out of a cucumber – these will be used for the irises.
4. Using a straw cut two circles out of the black pancake – these will be used for the pupils.
5. Using scissors cut two small strips with the remaining pancake – these will be used for the eyebrows.
6. Using a knife cut a strip the length of the width of the sausage roll out of the red capsicum – these will be used for the collar.
7. Once the sausage rolls are cooked place onto a plate, insert the ears into the roll in an upright position.
8. Place the flatbread eyes onto the round tip of the sausage roll – you can use a tiny amount of sauce as glue.
9. Place the cucumber irises onto the eyes.
10. Place the black pancake pupil onto each iris.
11. Place the flatbread element of shine onto the left side of each pupil.
12. Place the black pancake eyebrows above the eyes.
13. Place toothpick into the olive and insert it in between the eyes to create the nose.

Budgie
BAGEL

TIME
15 min

SERVES
1 People

DIFFICULTY
Easy

INGREDIENTS

STORE-BOUGHT BAGEL • HUMMUS (REFER TO HUMMUS RECIPE) • FLATBREAD • YELLOW CAPSICUM
RED CAPSICUM • CHERRY TOMATO • OLIVE • BLUEBERRIES • CARROT • CREAM CHEESE • BLACK PANCAKE
BLUEBERRIES

CREATION METHOD

1. Using scissors cut two round arches out of the flatbread (refer to image) these will be used for the eyes.

2. Using scissors cut the teeth out of the flatbread – refer to image.

3. Using a tiny cutter cut two circles out of the flatbread – these will be used to create the element of shine in the eye.

4. Using scissors cut smaller round arch shapes out of the black pancake (refer to image) this will be used for the pupils.

5. Using scissors cut a large round arch shape out of the black pancake – this will be used to create the mouth.

6. Using scissors cut around the edge of the pancake to create a strip – you will need one large one and two smaller ones for the eyebrows.

7. Using a knife cut a yellow capsicum in half. Then cut the shape of a cap out of it – refer to image.

8. Using a knife cut a jagged piece out of the red capsicum – refer to image for the shape – this will be used for the hair.

9. Using a knife cut a cherry tomato in half – this will be the tongue.

10. Using a tiny circle cutter cut three circles out of the slice of carrot – these will be used for the freckles.

11. Using a spoon place some cream cheese onto the bagel.

12. Using a separate spoon place hummus around the cream cheese and all over the remaining bagel. You can build up areas of the face such as the cheeks by adding more hummus in those areas.

13. Place the flatbread eyes onto the cream cheese.

14. Place the black pancake pupils on each of the flatbread eyes.

15. Place the flatbread element of shine circle on the right side of each pupil.

16. Place the larger black pancake strip vertically in between the two eyes.

17. Place the two smaller black pancake strips above the eyes.

18. Place the black pancake mouth on the bottom of the bagel.

19. Place the capsicum hair on the top part of the cream cheese.

20. Add the yellow capsicum cap onto of the hair.

21. Place the olive nose on below the eyes.

22. Place the cherry tomato tongue on the bottom of the mouth.

23. Place the flatbread teeth above the tongue.

24. Place blueberries along the edge of the bagel.

25. Place the carrots on the the cheek area.

Monster
MINESTRONE

TIME
60 min

SERVES
6+ People

DIFFICULTY
Intermediate

INGREDIENTS

3 LAMB SHANKS • I ONION • I ZUCCHINI • I CUP MUSHROOMS • I CUP FROZEN PEAS • 2 LARGE POTATOES
I CUP SPINACH • I CUP CELERY • I CARROT • I/2 BOTTLE PASSATA SAUCE • SEA SALT (TO TASTE)
PARMESAN CHEESE • PARSLEY (GARNISH) • I/2 PACKET OF PASTA • OLIVE OIL • FLATBREAD • BLACK PANCAKE

RECIPE

I. Dice the onion and place in a large pot with olive oil.

2. Sweat onion and add the shanks and the sliced mushrooms. Brown the shanks on each side.

3. Add enough water to the pot to fully cover the shanks, stir in passata add desired amount of sea salt and leave to cook on low heat for 2-3 hours.

4. Dice the vegetables and place aside until ready.

5. Add the zucchini, carrot, peas, spinach and allow to cook for 30 minutes.

6. Add the diced potatoes and cook for another 10 minutes.

7. Add the pasta and cook until al dente.

8. Place in bowl garnish with shaved parmesan and chopped parsley.

Monster ROLLS

TIME	**SERVES**	**DIFFICULTY**
30 min	8 Buns	Intermediate

INGREDIENTS

2 TBSP ACTIVE DRY YEAST • 1 CUP WARM WATER • 1/3 CUP OLIVE OIL • 1 EGG • 1 TSP SALT

4 CUPS WHOLEMEAL FLOUR • BLACK PANCAKE

RECIPE

1. Preheat over to 180c.
2. Combine water and yeast in a bowl and whisk until foamy.
3. Place flour in a large bowl, create a well in the middle and add the yeast mixture, oil and egg.
4. Gently fold the mixture until all ingredients are combined. Once combined use your hands to create a dough consistency. You may want to dust your hand with some flour first to avoid the dough sticking.
5. Dust your bench with some flour, place the dough onto the bench and knead for 2-3 minutes – do not let rise.
6. Divide the dough into 8 pieces.
7. Shape each part into an oval shape, using scissors snip around the edges. Place 6 cm apart on a greased baking tray.
8. Bake until for 12 minutes or until golden brown.

CREATION METHOD

1. Whilst bread to baking using an oval cutter cut two oval shapes out of the flatbread – these will be used for the eyes.
2. Using scissors cut two small triangles out of the remaining flatbread – these will be used for the teeth.
3. Using the tiny circle cutter, cut two circles out of the black pancake – these will be used for the pupils.
4. Using scissors cut a strip of pancake – this will be used for the mouth.
5. Place the eyes onto the bread.
6. Place the pupil black pancake circles on top of the eyes.
7. Place the black pancake strip under the eyes slightly curving it so that it looks sad.
8. Place the flatbread triangle teeth on each side of the mouth.

Dino
PESTO PASTA

TIME
30 min

SERVES
4 People

DIFFICULTY
Intermediate

INGREDIENTS

1 CUP KALE • 1 CUP SPINACH • 1/2 CUP MACADAMIA NUTS • 1/2 CUP OLIVE OIL • 1 LEMON
1 CUP SHAVED PARMESON • 1 PACKET PASTA • FLATBREAD • CUCUMBER • BLACK PANCAKE • 1 GARLIC
CLOVE • 1 CUCUMBER

RECIPE

1. Fill a pot with water and bring it to the boil.
2. Place kale, spinach, macadamia nuts, garlic, olive oil and parmesan in a food processor and blitz until a smooth consistency.
3. Once the water has boiled, place the spaghetti in the pot and cook until al dente.
4. In a pan add some olive oil and the pesto, allow it to simmer and stir occasionally.
5. Add some of the pasta water to the pesto and stir.
6. Drain the cooked pasta and mix through pesto.
7. Squeeze lemon onto the pasta.

CREATION METHOD

1. Whilst the pasta is cooking using a cookie cutter cut two circles out of the flatbread – these will be used for the eyes.
2. Using scissors cut 10 triangles out of the remaining flatbread – these will be used for the teeth.
3. Using the tiny circle cutter cut two circles out of flatbread – these will be used to create the element of shine in eyes.
4. Using a large pen lid cut two circles out of a the black pancake.

5. Using scissors cut a long strip around the edge of the pancake – this will be used for the eyes.
6. Using a knife cut the ends of the cucumber – you will need two slices – these will be used for the irises.
7. Using a knife cut two thick curved lines out of the cucumber – this will be used for the eyebrows.
8. Using a knife cut a triangle out of the remaining cucumber – this will be used for the spike.
9. Add pasta to a plate. Layer more around the bottom to create the snout – refer to image.
10. Place the flatbread eyes onto the top section of the face.
11. Place the cucumber iris on top of the flatbread.
12. Place the black pancake pupils onto of the cucumber iris.
13. Place the flatbread element of shine on the top left side of each pupil.
14. Place the cucumber eyebrows above each eye.
15. Place the strip of black pancake on the bottom section of the face – slightly curving to create a smile.
16. Using tweezers place a row of flatbread teeth below the mouth.
17. Place the cucumber spike on top of the head.

Fox
PUMPKIN SOUP

TIME
60 min

SERVES
4⁺ People

DIFFICULTY
Intermediate

INGREDIENTS

1 PUMPKIN • 1 ONION • 2 GARLIC CLOVES • 1 CARROT • OLIVE OIL • 2 CUPS MILK • SEA SALT • OLIVE OIL
FLATBREAD • 1 CHERRY TOMATO • BLACK PANCAKE • 1 BLACK OLIVE

RECIPE

1. Preheat oven to 160c.
2. Cut pumpkin and carrots in chunks and place in a tray with the garlic cloves. Cover with olive oil, sprinkle sea salt and place in oven until pumpkin is soft and roasted.
3. Once vegetables are cooked place into a food processor with milk and blitz until smooth.

CREATION METHOD

1. Whilst the vegetables are in the oven, using scissors cut a curved line halfway through a small flatbread.
2. With the remainder of the flatbread cut out two triangle shapes – refer to image – these will be used for the ears.
3. Place the ears and the flatbread into the oven and cook until it is a golden brown colour.
4. Using the tiny circle cutter cut two circles out of the flatbread – these will be used for the element of shine in the eye.
5. Using a pen lid slightly bend and cut two oval shapes out of the black pancake – these will be used for the eyes.
6. Using scissors cut along the edge of the pancake and create three strips – two will be used for the eyebrows, one will be used for the mouth.
7. Using a knife cut the cherry tomato in half – these will be used for the cheeks.
8. Once soup is in a bowl place the the curved flatbread onto the bottom of the bowl.
9. Place the black pancake eyes above the flatbread.
10. Place the flatbread element of shine circles on the left side of each pupil.
11. Place the black pancake eyebrows above the eyes.
12. Place and olive nose in the top-middle of the toasted flatbread.
13. Place a cherry tomato on each side of the nose.
14. Insert the ear on into the soup.

Star
CHICKEN NUGGETS

TIME	SERVES	DIFFICULTY
90 min	4+ People	Intermediate

INGREDIENTS

500G CHICKEN THIGH • 2 TBSP PLAIN FLOUR • I GARLIC CLOVE • I TBSP SEA SALT • I/2 CUP OLIVE OIL
2 SLICES OF TOAST • I EGG • OLIVE OIL TO FRY • FLATBREAD • I SMALL CUCUMBER • RED CAPSICUM
YELLOW CAPSICUM • CARROT • PURPLE CABBAGE • MAYONNAISE (OPTIONAL) • BLACK PANCAKE

RECIPE

1. Using a knife debone the chicken and place into a blender along with the garlic, flour, sea salt and olive oil and blend until a smooth paste consistency.

2. Place baking paper onto a plate and spread the chicken paste onto the plate, making sure to spread it evenly to the desired thickness. Place in freezer for 2 hours or until mixture is hard.

3. Toast two slices of bread and allow them to cool down then place in blender and blitz until it turns into crumbs. Place the crumbs onto a plate plate.

4. In a small bowl whisk the egg and place aside.

5. Remove the chicken paste from the freezer. Using the star cutter cut out as many stars as you can.

6. Place the star nuggets into the egg wash making sure they are covered, then place them down onto the breadcrumbs. Turn on the other side so that both sides are fully crumbed.

7. Place olive oil in frying pan, once the oil has heated place the nuggets and cook on each side until golden brown. Place onto paper towel to drain the excess oil.

CREATION METHOD

1. Using a pen lid cut two circles out of the flatbread – these will be used for the eyes.

2. Using a tiny circle cutter cut two circles out of the remaining flatbread – these will be used to create the element of shine in the eye.

3. Using a pen lid cut two circles out of a slice of cucumber – these will be used for the irises.

4. Using a pen lid cut two circles out of the black pancake – these will be used for the pupils.

5. Using scissors cut a small strip along the edge of the black pancake – this will be used to create the mouth.

6. Cut all the vegetables into strips.

7. Place the flatbread eyes onto the top of the nugget.

8. Place the cucumber irises onto the eyes.

9. Place the black pancake pupils onto the cucumber irises.

10. Place the flatbread elements of shine circles onto the left side of each black pancake pupil.

11. Place the black pancake strip below the eyes.

12. Place the vegetables onto the plate.

13. Optional – dab a small amount of mayonnaise or tomato sauce below each eye to create the cheeks

Sarah Says

Leap across the rainbow and jump in the air as you star jump everywhere.

DINNER

Dahl
ROOSTER

TIME	SERVES	DIFFICULTY
60 min	4+ People	Intermediate

INGREDIENTS

500G RED LENTILS • 1 ONION • 4 CLOVES GARLIC • 1 TSP GINGER • 1 TBSP CURRY POWDER • 1 TBSP TURMERIC
1 CARROT • 1 POTATO • 2 TBSP TOMATO PASTE • 1/4 CUP CORIANDER • 1/4 PARSLEY • OLIVE OIL • SEA SALT • 2 CUPS
GLUTINOUS RICE • 1/2 RED & YELLOW CAPSICUM • 1/4 CUP SPINACH • CARROT • CUCUMBER • BLACK PANCAKE • FLATBREAD

RECIPE

1. Grate the carrot and potato.
2. Finely chop the parsley and coriander.
3. Finely dice onion and add to a pot with some olive oil, fry until golden brown, add garlic.
4. Add curry powder, turmeric, salt, tomato paste, grate ginger and stir for 2 minutes on a low heat.
5. Wash the red lentils and add to pot, stir for 5 minutes on low.
6. Add 5 cups of water, carrot, potato, parsley and coriander and stir. Leave to cook for one hour making sure to stir regularly.

CREATION METHOD

1. Cook the rice and set aside to cool.
2. Using a knife slice the ends of a cucumber to create two circles – these will be used for the irises.
3. Using a large pen lid cut two circles out of the black pancake.
4. Using a tiny circle cutter, cut two circles out of the flatbread – these will be used to create an element of shine.
5. For the beak, cut the tip of a carrot and peel the skin. Using a toothpick insert two holes at the top to create the nostrils.
6. Using a knife cut the shape of the rooster's comb and wattle out of red capsicum.
7. Using a knife cut the yellow capsicum and cut the purple cabbage into slices.
8. Using scissors cut cling wrap in a square shape. Place 2 tbsp of cooked rice in the middle and bring bring corner of the glad wrap to the centre and twist. Shape the rice into a ball. Repeat. These will be used for the eyes.
9. Remove the cling wrap and place the rice balls on the plate.
10. Using a spoon gently place a small amount of dahl in between the eyes and on the bottom of the plate.
11. Place the purple cabbage above the dahl.
12. Place the spinach above the purple cabbage.
13. Place the yellow capsicum above the spinach.
14. Place the wattle on top of the yellow capsicum.
15. Place the beak above the wattle.
16. Place the comb slightly above the beak.
17. Place the cucumber on each rice ball.
18. Place the black pancake pupils onto each cucumber.
19. Place the flatbread element of shine circles on the top left side of each black pancake to create an element of shine.

Fish
GOUJANS

TIME
60 min

SERVES
4⁺ People

DIFFICULTY
Advanced

INGREDIENTS

500G FISH OF YOUR CHOICE • 1 CUP CORNFLAKES • 1 EGG • FLATBREAD • CHERRY TOMATOES • CARROTS CUCUMBER • PURPLE CABBAGE • BLACK PANCAKE • MAYONNAISE

RECIPE

1. Cut fish into bite-size pieces.
2. In a small bowl whisk an egg and place aside.
3. Place the cornflakes into a food processor and blitz until crumbs, place the crumbs on a plate.
4. Dip the pieces of fish in the egg and then place onto the crumbs. Make sure fish is covered with crumbs on both sides.
5. Place some olive oil in frying pan and once oil has heated place pieces of fish and allow to cook. Cook until golden brown on each side. Place onto paper towel to soak up excess oil.

CREATION METHOD

1. Using a small cookie cutter cut one circle out of a piece of flatbread – this will be used to create the eyes.
2. Using a straw cut a circle out of the remaining flatbread – this will be used to create an element of shine.
3. Using a knife slice the cucumber into circles – place one aside for the eye, the rest will be used for the scales.
4. Using a pen lid cut a circle out of the black pancake – this will be used for the pupil.

5. Using scissors cut around the edge of the black pancake to create a strip – this will be used for the fish's eyelash.
6. Using scissors cut round arches out of a leaf of purple cabbage.
7. Slice a carrot to create circles.
8. Place the fish bites in a shape to create the head, tail and fins. Make sure to leave a gap in the middle for the vegetables – refer to image.
9. Start with the cucumber, layer them in a line, then add the purple cabbage scales, then carrots, then cherry tomatoes.
10. Add the flatbread circles onto of the head section.
11. Place the cucumber iris onto the eye.
12. Place the black pancake pupil onto the cucumber.
13. Place the flatbread element of shine on the top left side of the eye.
14. Place a small fish bite onto the eye to create an eyelid.
15. Gently place the black pancake line along the bottom of the eyelid.
16. Using a small spoon, place a few dabs of mayonnaise onto the plate and swirl in circular motion to create circles.

The Enchanted Oak Tree
LAMB SHANKS, MASH & BROCCOLI

TIME
60 min

SERVES
4 People

DIFFICULTY
Intermediate

INGREDIENTS

**2 LAMB SHANKS • SALT • PEPPER • OLIVE OIL • IKG MASHED POTATOES • 50G BUTTER • I/4 CUP MILK
SEA SALT & PEPPER • BROCCOLINI • CHERRY TOMATOES • FLATBREAD • BLACK PANCAKE**

RECIPE

1. Preheat oven to 180c.
2. Place some oil in tray and add shanks. Massage shanks with a generous amount of oil, sea salt to desired taste and pepper.
3. Place in oven and allow to cook for approx 2 hours or until meat falls off the bone.

CREATION METHOD

1. Cut potatoes into quarters and place in a pot, cover with water and allow to cook until potatoes are soft.
2. Strain potatoes and add butter, milk and salt and mash until a smooth consistency.
3. Using a pen lid cut two circles out of black pancake.
4. Using scissors cut around the edge of the black pancake to create a strip – this will be used for the mouth
5. Using scissors cut two curved rectangle shapes out of the flatbread – these will be used for the eyes – don't worry too much about it being perfect as they will mainly be covered later
6. Using a tiny circle cutter cut two circles out of the remaining flatbread.
7. Place the mashed potato on the plate, roughly create a shape of the Enchanted Oak Tree including the nose.
8. Place the flatbread eyes on each side of the nose.
9. Place the black pancake pupils in the middle of each eye.
10. Place the flatbread element of shine onto each black pancake pupil.
11. Shred the shanks and place it all over the mashed potato tree, gently press down to shape it.
12. Place the black pancake strip below the nose.
13. Place some steamed broccolini on the tops of the branches.
14. To make some flowers cut some cherry tomatoes in half and place along the root of the tree.

Hedgehog
CHICKEN CURRY PIE

TIME
90 min

SERVES
5 People

DIFFICULTY
Intermediate

INGREDIENTS

600G DICED CHICKEN THIGH • 5 SHEETS PUFF PASTRY • 1 ONION • 1 GARLIC GLOVE • 1 CARROT • 1 CUP GREEN PEAS
1 CUP CORN KERNELS • 2 POTATOES • 1 CUP SPINACH • 1/2 CUP CHICKEN STOCK • 1 TSP CURRY POWDER
SEA SALT • 2 WHITE QUINOA SEEDS • FLATBREAD • CUCUMBER • BLACK PANCAKE

RECIPE

1. Preheat oven to 160c.
2. Dice onions and fry with some olive oil until golden brown, add garlic and curry powder.
3. Add the diced chicken and fry until cooked.
4. Dice potatoes and add to the mixture.
5. Add the remaining vegetables and chicken stock and allow to simmer until liquid is reduced.
6. Add desired amount of sea salt, place aside to cool.
7. Place a ramekin onto the sheet of puff pastry and cut around it with the knife.
8. Place the mixture into the ramekin and cover with the puff pastry.
9. Using scissors cut a smaller semicircle and stick it on the front of the pie to create the face.
10. Using scissors cut two little ears and two little paws and place them onto the pie – refer to image.
11. Using scissors cut little snippets into the body to create a fur-like effect.
12. Roll a small ball with the scrap bit of puff pastry and stick onto the face for the nose.
13. Place in the oven for 40 minutes or until golden brown.

CREATION METHOD

1. Using a large pen lid cut two circles out of piece of flatbread – these will used for the eyes.
2. Using a pen lid cut two circles out of a slice of cucumber – these will be used for the irises.
3. Using a tiny circle cutter cut two circles out of the black pancake.
4. Using scissors cut three small strips out of the black pancake – these will be used for the eyebrows and mouth.
5. Once the pie is cooked brush a small amount of oil onto the flatbread eye and stick it onto the face.
6. Place the cucumber irises onto the flatbread eyes.
7. Place the black pancake onto the cucumber iris.
8. Dip knife into some water and press onto the quinoa seed so that it sticks onto the knife. Using a toothpick gently push the quinoa seed on to the left side of each black pancake pupil to create an element of shine.
9. Place a black pancake eyebrow above each eye.
10. Place a black pancake strip below the nose for the mouth.

SWEET POTATO GNOCCHI

TIME
90 min

SERVES
4 People

DIFFICULTY
Advanced

INGREDIENTS

500G POTATOES • 500G SWEET POTATOES • 1 EGG • 2 CUPS SPELT FLOUR • BUTTER • 1 BOTTLE PASSATA SAUCE
1 ONION • 1 ZUCCHINI • 1 CARROT • 1 CUP MUSHROOMS • 1 CUP SPINACH • SEA SALT • BLACK PANCAKE • 1
CUCUMBER • 1 CHERRY TOMATO

RECIPE

Gnocchi

1. Peel potatoes and sweet potato, cut into cubes and put into a pot of water to boil.
2. Once cooked remove and mash.
3. Dust the bench with some flour.
4. Place potato onto the bench and allow to cool, make a well in the middle and the egg.
5. Slowly add the flour and fold until a smooth consistency.
6. Roll the gnocchi mixture into a tube-like shape and using a knife cut into little bite-size rectangles.
7. Boil water in a pot, once water is bubbling gently add the pieces of gnocchi into the water. When the gnocchi starts to float it is ready to be removed. Set aside to cool down.
8. Add butter to a pan, once the butter is melted pan-fry each gnocchi until golden brown on each side.

Sauce

1. Grate the mushrooms, zucchini and carrots.
2. Add chopped onion into a pan with some olive oil.
3. Add the mushroom, zucchini and carrot, stir for a few mintues.
4. Add the passata sauce, salt and 1 cup of water and stir, leave sauce to cook and reduce for 30 minutes, occasionally stirring.

CREATION METHOD

1. Using scissors cut the shape of the eyes out of flatbread.
2. Using a straw cut two circles out of the remaining flatbread – these will be used to create the element of shine in the eyes.
3. Using a knife cut two slices off the ends of the cucumber – these will be used for the irises.
4. Using a large pen lid cut two circles out of the black pancake – these will be used for the pupils.
5. Using scissors cut around the edge of the pancake to create two strips – these will be used for the mouth.
6. Place sauce onto plate and spread into a lion mane shape.
7. Place the gnocchi onto the sauce in the shape of a lion.
8. Place a few gnocchis on top of the bottom section of the face to create the snout.
9. Place one piece of gnocchi on the top of each side for the ears.
10. Place the flatbread eyes onto the face.
11. Place the cucumber irises onto the flatbread eyes.
12. Place the black pancake pupils onto the cucumber.
13. Place the flatbread element of shine onto the left side of each pupil.
14. Place a cherry tomato on top of the snout for the nose.
15. Place the two strip of black pancake below mouth making sure to curve it at the ends to create a smile.
16. Cut a gnocchi in half and place each piece above an above to create the eyebrows.

SNACKS

Hummus Veggie Patch

INGREDIENTS

1 can chickpeas • 1 garlic glove • 1 lemon • Sea salt • 2tbsp tahini • Dutch carrots • Small capsicums • Lettuce • Flatbread Cucumber

RECIPE

1. Drain the chickpeas pour into blender along with the garlic, tahini and sea salt to taste.
2. Squeeze a lemon and bltiz until smooth consistency.
3. Add more lemon juice if needed, place in fridge.

CREATION METHOD

1. Preheat oven to 150c.
2. Using scissors cut spade shapes out of flatbread – refer to image. Place in oven for 2-3 minutes.
3. Place hummus in a bowl, place desired vegetables on top of hummus, serve with spades.

Little Boy Blue Smoothie

INGREDIENTS

1 banana • 1/4 cup frozen blueberries • 1tbsp raw honey • 1tsp chia seeds • 1 1/2 cups milk

RECIPE

1. Place all ingredients in a blender and blitz.
2. Pour in cup.

Granola Cups

INGREDIENTS

2 cups oats • 1/2 cup raw honey • 1/2 tbsp coconut oil • 1/2 cup nuts • 1/2 cup sultanas • 1/2 cup chia seeds • 1/2 cup goji berries • 1/2 cup shredded coconut

RECIPE

1. Preheat oven to 180c.
2. In a pot add coconut oil, once the oil has melted mix in the honey and cook until it starts to bubble.
3. In a large bowl mix all the ingredient except for the sultanas.
4. Add the coconut oil and honey mixture and mix through.
5. Place in a tray and in the oven for 7 minutes.
6. Remove from oven and mix in sultanas – leave to cool down and granola to harden.
7. Serve with yoghurt and fruit.

Hedgehog Protein Balls

INGREDIENTS

1 cup oats • 1 tbsp cocoa powder • 1/4 cup chia seeds • 1/2 cup crushed cashews • 1/2 cup shredded coconut • 1/4 cup coconut oil Slithered almonds • Sultanas • Black pancake

RECIPE

1. In a blender add oats and quinoa seeds and blitz until it turns into powder.
2. Add into a large bowl, add in chia seeds, crushed cashews, coconut and goji berries and mix .
3. In a small pot melt the coconut oil and add the honey and stir until the mixture bubbles.
4. Remove and mix and using your hand roll out into small balls.

CREATION METHOD

1. nsert the almond slithers to create spikes.
2. Snap an almond slither in half to create the eyes.
3. Place a sultana below the eyes to create the nose.
4. Using a tiny circle cutter, cut two circles out of the black pancake.
5. Place balls into fridge and allow to harden.

Honey Joys Chicken

INGREDIENTS

2 cups cornflakes • 1/2 cup raw honey • 1/4 cup oconut oil
1 strawberry • 1 black pancake • 1 almond

RECIPE

1. Preheat oven to 160c.
2. Melt coconut oil in a pot, once melted add honey and stir still it bubbles.
3. Pour coconut mixture into bowl and mix evenly.
4. Place honey joy mixture into patty pans and place in oven for 10-15 minutes.
5. Remove and place in the fridge until hardened.

CREATION METHOD

1. Using a knife cut the wattle and crown shape out of the strawberry
2. Using a straw cut two circles out of the black pancake – these will be used for the eyes.
3. Once the honey joys have hardened place the eyes in the honey joy.
4. Place and almond in the middle of the eyes to create the beak.
5. Place the wattle strawberry below the almond.

Black
PANCAKE

TIME
10 min

SERVES
1+ People

DIFFICULTY
Easy

INGREDIENTS

1/4 CUP FLOUR • WATER • BLACK FOOD DYE

RECIPE

1. Place flour and food dye in a small bowl
2. Add enough cold water and stir so that the consistency is of a pancake/crepe batter
3. Place some oil onto a pan and pour small amounts of batter
4. Allow batter to cook through, but do not flip the pancake
5. Remove and place on a plate and into the fridge to cool down

The Stories
THAT INSPIRED THE RECIPES

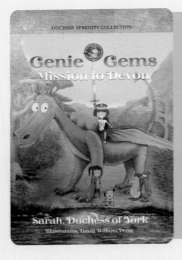

Genie Gems: Mission to Devon

INSPIRED

1. Genie Gems Dragon toast
2. Genie Gems Princess Toast
3. Genie Gems Omelettes
4. Dino Pesto Pasta

Genie Gems: Meets Arthur Fantastic

INSPIRED

1. Genie Gems Princess Toast
2. Arthur Fantastic Scones
3. Genie Gems Omlettes
4. Lion Sweet Potato Gnocchi

Budgie the Helicoper Rescues Kubbie the Koala

INSPIRED

1. Budgie Bagel

Budgie and the Dronenaughts

INSPIRED

1. Budgie Bagel

The Enchanted Oak Tree

INSPIRED

1. Lamb Shanks mash & broccoli

About
FOOD ARTIST

May 2015, Laleh turned her son Jacob's spelt pancake into a lion- he absolutely loved it and Jacob's Food Diaries was born!

Within a month her creations went viral gaining worldwide media attention including Good Morning America, CBS, Ellen, ABC, The Today Show, Sunrise, Martha Stewart and many more.

Jacob's Food Diaries has become a global success allowing Laleh to collaborate with major production companies including Disney, Netflix, Nickelodeon, Universal Pictures, 20th Century Fox, The Food Network and Jamie Oliver.

With followers around the world including celebrities such as Gigi Hadid, Miranda Kerr, Jimmy Kimmel, Jamie Oliver and Stacey Solomon, Jacob's Food Diaries is a platform for everyone to enjoy!

About
THE AUTHOR

Sarah, Duchess of York is a global humanitarian, businesswoman, bestselling children's book author, producer and wellness advocate.

The Duchess has published over 80 books including two autobiographies and titles dealing with health, empowerment, history, art, as well as many children's stories.

Sarah's Trust is an international charity founded to share aid to those in need through resources and kindness.
www.sarahstrust.com